I0157301

Trip 65

Misadventures in Four Languages

By Bernard Catalinotto

2024

Trip 65

Misadventures in Four Languages

Bernard Catalinotto

Copyright ©2024 by Bernard Catalinotto

ISBN13 # 979-8-9872176-3-4

Travel adventures 1965, Coming of age memoir, Kuwait, Iraq, Syria, Jordan, Israel, Greece, Italy, Austria, Germany, France, and USA.

Maps are the work of the author and are included in the copyright.

Publisher: FourPiRsquared, New York, N.Y., USA.

Email: fourpirsquaredbooks@gmail.com

Preface and Acknowledgments

This memoir is a collection of several short travel memoirs that I wrote in Diane Frank's creative writing courses at OLLI San Francisco State and OLLI Dominican College, Flash Fiction and Memoir.

A portion of the sections set in Sicily, "Sicily Excursion 1965," was published in the online literary magazine, *Vistas and Byways*, by OLLI San Francisco State University in Spring, 2021.

I'd like to thank my wonderful teacher Diane for her encouragement and many excellent editorial suggestions, without which I would never have had the courage to publish this work. I'd also like to thank the other students in the class, many of whom gave great suggestions.

I'd like to thank my wife, Roberta; brother John, sister Ann, sister-in-law Ellen and brother-in-law John for their encouragement and many good editorial suggestions, especially my brother John's sage advice on "Cinema Paradiso" and "Across the Dolomites."

Contents

Maps

1. Trip 65 Overview

2. Middle East

3. Jerusalem / Gethsemane

4. Jerusalem / Jericho

5. Israel / West Bank

6. Israel / Lake Tiberias / Syria

7. Israel / Haifa

8. Greece from East to West

9. Sicily

10. Italy from South to North

11 Northern Italy / Austria

12 New York State

NY

Paris
train
WEST GERMANY
FRANCE
Munich
SW
AUSTRIA
ITALY
4
3
Venice
Rome
YUGOSLAVIA
Palermo
GREECE
boat
TURKEY
IRAQ
Athens
SYRIA
boat
Beirut
car
Kuwait
1

1 Haifa
2 Messina
3 Florence
4 Maniago

Jerusalem
JORDAN

EGYPT

Map 1. Trip 65 Overview

Across the Crescent

I graduated from Columbia in sixty-four and worked that summer at the Kuwait Student Bureau in New York City, where I met a charismatic Iraqi entrepreneur who offered me a well-paid job researching new businesses for his investment company in Kuwait. The job was engaging for a few months, but the new businesses did not materialize, so I decided to leave. This is the story of my adventures in Arabic, French, Italian and English while homeward bound. They started one morning in June 1965 in a working class neighborhood of Kuwait City.

I met my friend Andreas, his older sister, her husband, and their daughter outside their apartment at dawn and squeezed into the rear seat of the sedan. For one-fifth the gas money, I would spend the next twenty-four hours with Andreas's family, driving with him across the Fertile Crescent. We passed the Kuwait Yacht Club as the sun shone red through the dust over the Gulf. After nine months in the sandbox, I was going home.

I was only a little sad to leave Kuwait. It had been an adventure, my first real job out of college six thousand miles from home. But I had nothing to do at work, and Hussam's crackpot scheme to get rich had fizzled. Maryam, my local girlfriend, was thankfully still a virgin, but the influx of college girls on summer break was overly tempting. I also had to check my mail in Paris to make sure my draft board was still quiescent. So, I was mainly happy to be on my way.

We drove past Basra and floored it on the road to Baghdad. Then we headed west along the Tigris, where each town resembled a movie set of a Mexican town in the US Southwest. When the river shriveled to a stream, we reached the border, and I slept as we drove all night across the rocky Syrian desert. Suddenly, I awoke. We were parked near an ornate building that could have been in Paris. This must be Damascus, I thought, reassured, and fell back asleep. We crossed the mountains and arrived in Beirut for breakfast.

It was my second time in Lebanon. During my first trip, with my eyes acclimated to the dull tans and browns of the desert, the deep green hills of Cedar had pulsed with energy. I had visited an American businessman for Easter, staying at his posh house in the hills above Beirut. He proudly confided that he was sending his seventeen-year-old daughter to school in the States to prevent attachments to the perilously handsome and charming locals.

Andreas spoke fluent Greek, Arabic and English, all with the same native Greek accent. He found me a room at the American University on the waterfront, and I took him to the Corniche near the Pigeon Rocks, where we celebrated our return to civilization with a table of eggplant, squash, lamb, hummus, and baba ghanoush. He showed me around town, not that he really knew the town. He mistakenly put us on a bus to Baalbek's Roman ruins that was for tourists.

Map 2. Middle East

At first annoyed, we soon enjoyed the novelty of the refreshingly clueless Americans on summer holiday.

Back in town, I upset Andreas's cousin by guessing her age at thirty. She was only twenty, she said, and I felt bad for hurting her feelings. She seemed close to her family, a good girl, a Greek version of my distant cousins or the other protected Sicilian American girls I'd met at home. Attractive, but off limits.

The next day I flew to East Jerusalem, on the Jordanian side. I was ready to see the Holy Land and open to misadventure.

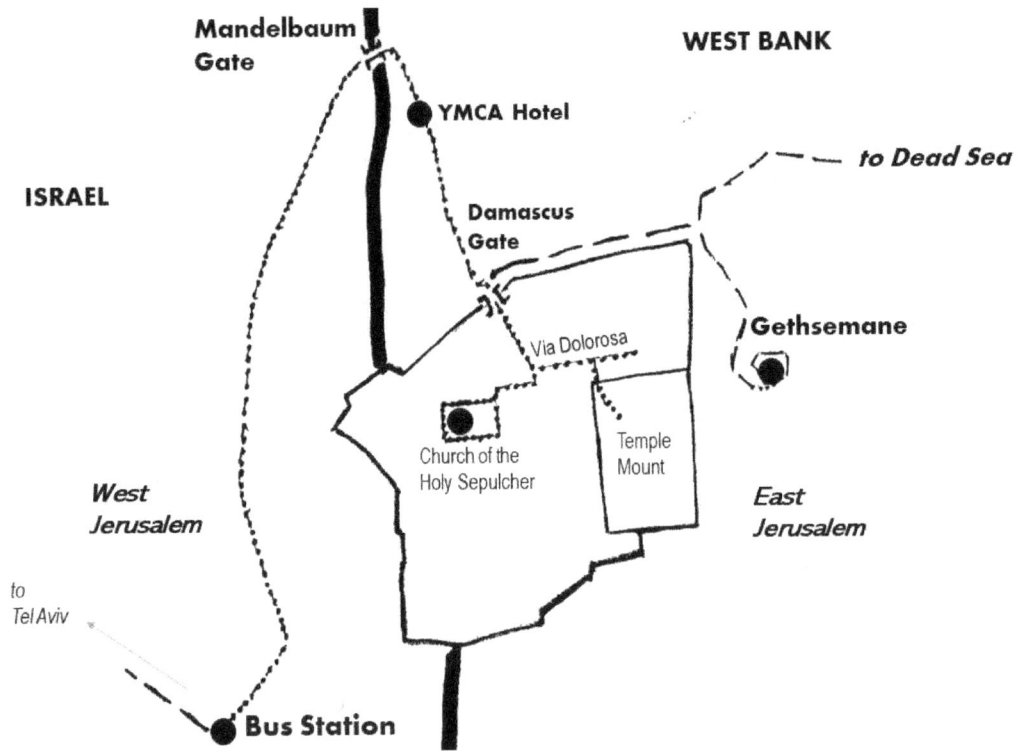

Map 3. Jerusalem / Gethsemane

My Battle of Jericho

I checked into the YMCA near the Old City and walked along the narrow Via Dolorosa to the Church of the Holy Sepulcher. Back at the Damascus Gate, I arranged for a taxi driver to take me to the Dead Sea, twenty miles east, wait for me, and drive me back to Jerusalem for twenty riyals. He drove me east across the desert, where an elderly American priest had wandered off and died of exposure and dehydration a few weeks earlier, and we reached the Dead Sea. I floated on the highly salted water in the lowest spot on earth, some fourteen hundred feet below sea level. The water was incredibly buoyant.

On the way back we were chatting in Arabic (his fluent, mine broken) and the driver turned around from the front of the car and slowed down to a crawl. He said he used to be friends with a Jewish Palestinian man his age. He would go to his friend's house and his friend would come to his house, but after the war with Israel, that friendship ended. He stared at me while the car was rolling forward slowly.

I asked politely, "Please, O God, we go, we return to Jerusalem."

He became angry and said, "You are for the Israelis."

I was shocked, and I didn't know what to say. I didn't want to protest too much, so I said simply, "I want that I return to Jerusalem."

He said he would take me to the police station in the nearby town of Jericho.

My stomach clenched. I was afraid my American passport might not protect me.

He said he would take me to Jerusalem, but only if I paid him another twenty riyals.

I relaxed. He only wanted money.

I called his bluff. I told him, "Let's go. We go to the police station, and we speak to them there."

He drove me into what looked to me like a Mexican border town with empty dirt streets and up to the police station. He spoke to them in their mother tongue, and I spoke to them in my Tarzan Arabic. I did not know the word for liar, so I said, "He says the thing that it is not true." He repeated his offer to take me to Jerusalem for another twenty riyals, and I asked the police "Where is the station for the autobus?"

I rode back on the bus with the locals and the chickens and decided I got a better deal since it was more authentic to ride the bus. And he got the minor satisfaction of dumping an American in Jericho, but not the greater satisfaction of ripping me off.

JORDAN

★ Jericho
2● ●1   1 police station
         2 bus stop

WEST BANK

bus   taxi

Sea level

River Jordan

ISRAEL

bus   taxi

Damascus
Gate

Discussion with
taxi driver

taxi

Jerusalem

Beach

Dead Sea

(elevation 1400 ft
below sea level)

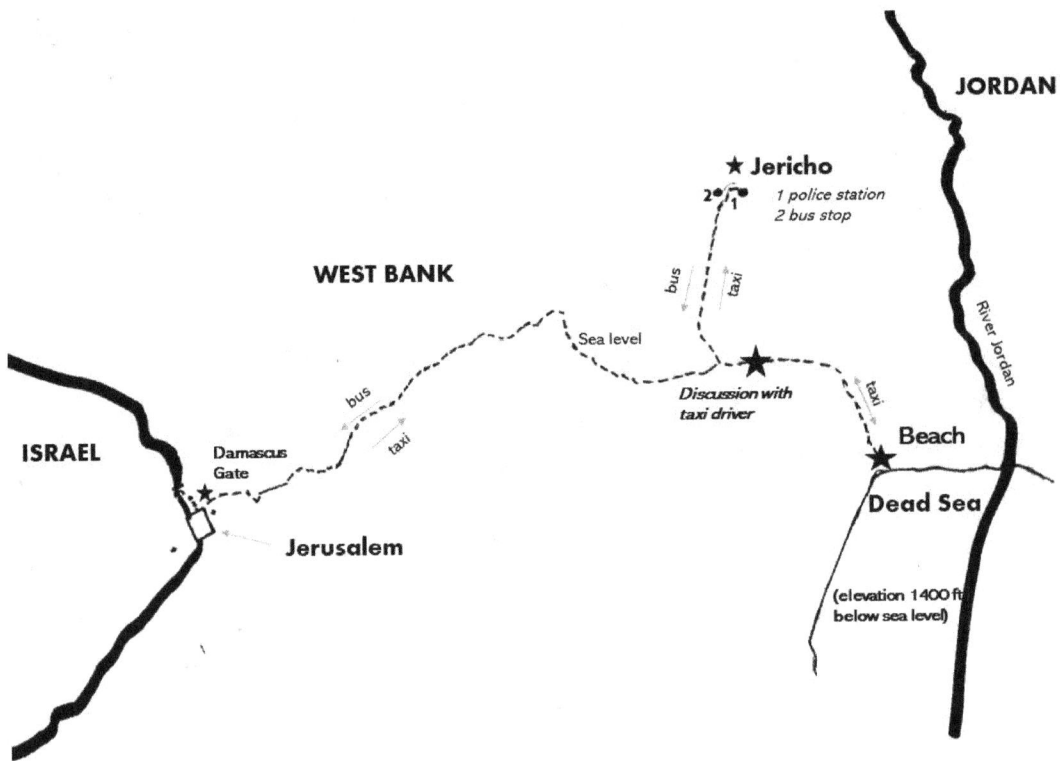

Map 4. Jerusalem / Jericho

I am a Spy

Back in town, I was eager to visit Gethsemane, the garden where according to legend, Jesus was arrested by the Romans after he was fingered by Judas Iscariot, who kissed him. I walked along the hillside road to the east of the Old City and fell into chatting with a young well-spoken Palestinian. I was tired of being thought an imperialist Zionist because I was American, so when he asked me what country I was from, I told him I was Italian.

He asked about the political situation in Italy, whether the Israelis or the Palestinians had the support of the people. I thought "Maybe it was not such a great idea to tell a patriotic Palestinian that I was something I am not." If he found out that I was lying and was as emotional as my Dead Sea taxi driver, he'd probably think I was a spy, which could be unpleasant.

He said he thought that Italians were sympathetic to the Israelis because their newspapers gave more favorable propaganda to the Israelis and did not report fairly about the Palestinians. That sounded plausible, but I had no idea how the Italian newspapers reported on the Middle East, so I told him that I'm not sure.

He seemed surprised and peered at me suspiciously.

"Who is the premier of Italy?"

Uh-oh. I did not know the answer but pulled "Moro" out of the air.

To my relief, that was the correct answer and we soon parted.

When my sons asked me years later if I ever did stupid things when I was their age, I gave this encounter as an example of one of the stupidest. It reminded me of an incident when some older Iraqi colleagues took me to a cafe in downtown Kuwait earlier that year. To show off my French, I chatted with a Syrian guy I had just met. He gave me a cunning smile and said I must be a spy to be living in Kuwait and spending time in the old quarter. Instead of denying it, I said, "You are right, I am a spy."

Nothing happened, but afterwards my colleague Hussam was very angry. "You are a stupid naive child," he said. "He might think you really are a spy because you admitted to being a spy. You cannot joke with them." Maybe I should have taken that lesson more to heart.

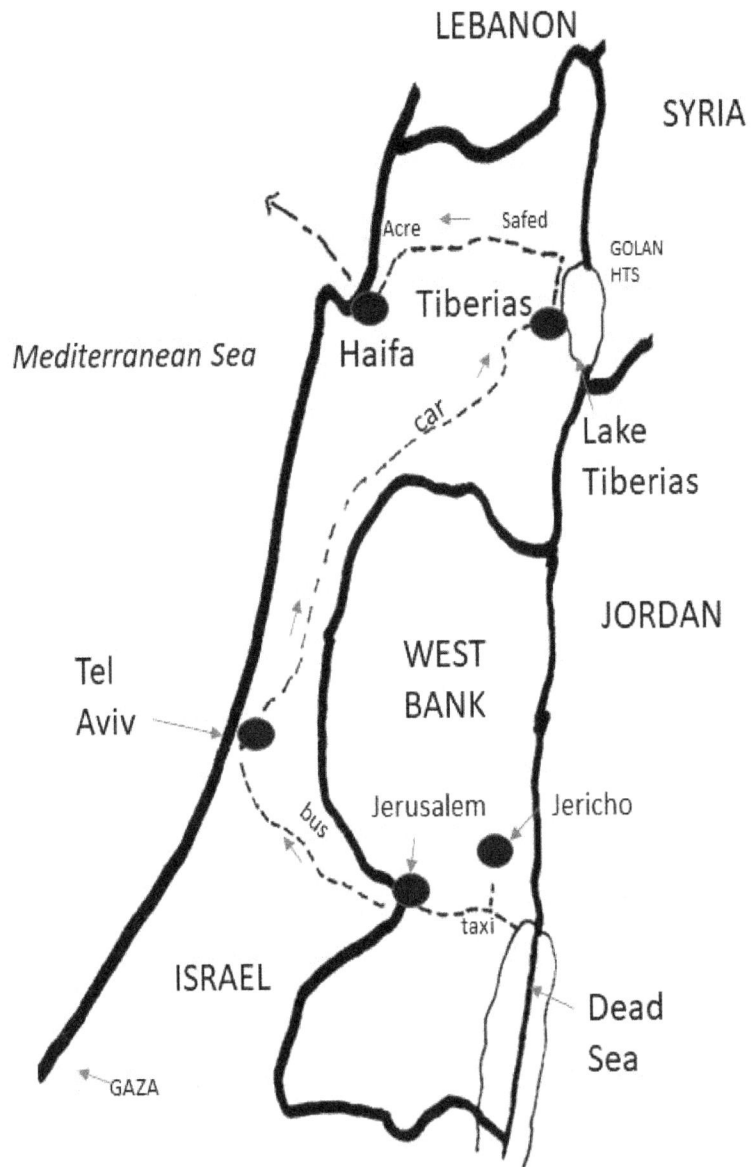

Map 5. Israel / West Bank

Through the Gate

The border guard slammed his huge stamp on my passport, posting JERUSALEM on a full page to assure no reentry. I eagerly strolled through the gate, passing from the Middle Ages to what I had been led to believe would be the twentieth century on the Israeli side. I boarded a bus from the dusty Jerusalem bus station, chatted with a friendly young woman on the bus, and debarked in the dusty Tel Aviv bus station. Yes, it was the twentieth century.

I was eager to visit a kibbutz. I'd heard about them as a fascinating social experiment and did not want to miss an opportunity to see one. I found a kibbutz that accepted visitors to supplement revenue from olives and turkeys. I asked the guide if it was true that they separate children from parents. He showed me the houses where the children slept and the nearby cabins where the parents slept – not a bad idea.

The next day I booked a car and drove north out of Tel Aviv. I had twenty-four hours until my boat sailed from Haifa. I'd wanted to see Lake Tiberias since childhood, where, in my six-year old's imagination, I conflated Jesus with Buck Rogers, who was fighting to destroy the evil genius Hitler, who lived in a castle at the northern end of the lake. That was where Jesus had walked on water.

The road was full of hitchhikers. I picked up a high school kid on his way home to Tiberias. He told me that as a baby, he escaped from Iraq in a basket over the mountains by donkey. I didn't have the heart to share that I'd made the same trip last week by car.

We approached Tiberias on an escarpment and saw the entire lake as we drove for miles, winding down to the lakeside city below. While in town, we met two American girls from Queens College in my hometown New York. One wanted to get in the car with us, but her friend preferred a trio of fast-talking Israeli guys. It was no contest.

My passenger directed us to a small beach on the lake. I removed my shoes and walked in but not on the water and then dropped him off by his parents' apartment.

Leaving Tiberias, I picked up a worried teenager returning to his kibbutz on the border with Syria, north of the lake. There had been a shelling from the Golan Heights. We pulled over by a police barricade at his turnoff. I offered to drive him the next mile home, but he said it was dangerous and insisted he go alone.

What's wrong with them, I thought. How can they put up with this?

Safed •

To Haifa

Kibbutz

Syrian Army
Cannons

Kibbutznik
drop off

Capernaum

Walk on water
site

Golan Heights
(Syria)

Israel

**Lake
Tiberias**

From Tel Aviv

escarpment

Tiberias

SYRIA

ISRAEL

JORDAN

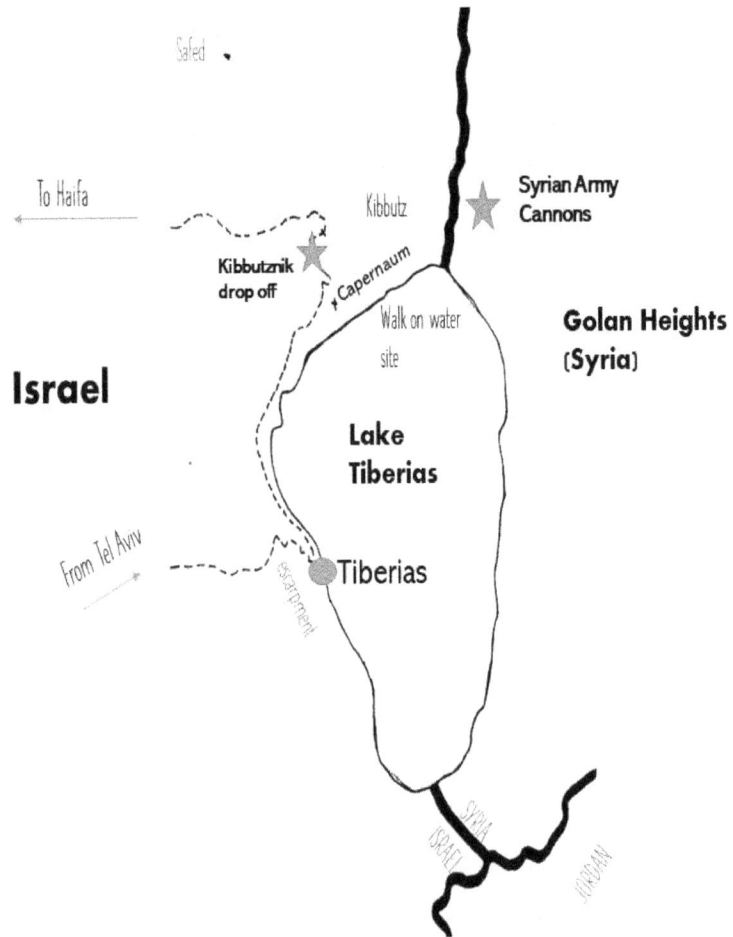

Map 6. Israel / Lake Tiberias / Syria

I was near the magical town of Safed and later passed the fascinating Crusader Castle at Acre. But on that day I knew nothing about them, so I raced past them on the road to Haifa and dropped my rental car at the port. I paid in advance for a dark hotel room on the waterfront and took the funicular railway to the city's upper level. I sat in the clean lobby of the fancy Dan Carmel Hotel, where a room cost a budget busting fifty-five dollars. It was the last night of my nine-month adventure in the exotic Middle East, so I took the room, took a long bath, and started to doze.

Did I dream it? Around two a.m. a motorcyclist zoomed up to the hotel entrance, and a young woman jumped off the bike and bid him a smiling good night. The image of her carefree "good night" stayed with me for years.

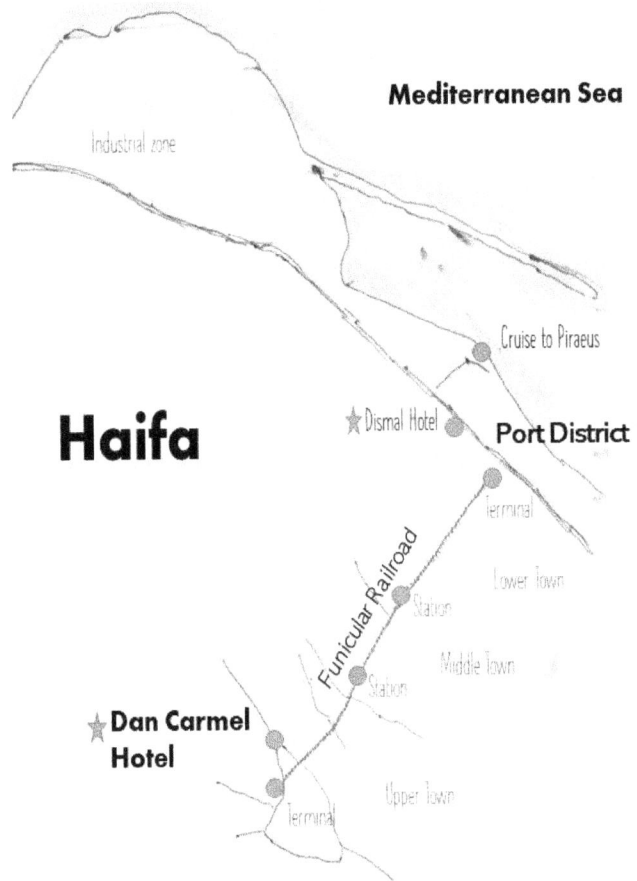

Mediterranean Sea

Industrial zone

Cruise to Piraeus

★ Dismal Hotel

Port District

Haifa

Terminal

Lower Town

Funicular Railroad

Station

Middle Town

★ **Dan Carmel Hotel**

Station

Upper Town

Terminal

Map 7. Israel / Haifa

Greece from East to West

The two young Israelis were giddy with joy to be out of the Army and made perfect dinner companions on the boat. After nine months in the Middle East, I went along when they ordered the pork, forbidden to Arab and Jew. I enjoyed watching them eat. They ate like they were making love to it, grinning, saying how wonderful it tasted.

I felt great relaxing on a cruise ship out of Haifa, destination Sicily, where I could visit some distant relatives and test my aunts' family legends. But first I had a stopover, my first visit to Athens.

In Piraeus we had free digs on the boat, so I dutifully headed for the Parthenon. I was eager to practice my schoolboy Italian, so I was happy when I met an Italian college kid studying in Athens. He was planning to take a bus to a modest seaside restaurant and invited me along. I gazed down from the bus at the boaters swimming next to their sailboats in the bright blue Mediterranean. I felt enchanted and even a little envious.

The restaurant was plain, a shack, which is what I was hoping for. The fish was white and delicate, fresh from the sea, sauteed with magic Greek spices, the best I'd ever had.

Back in town, I strolled along the main street in the Plaka, the neighborhood near the Parthenon with restaurants and hotels. It felt like a million miles from New York, so I was shocked to see someone I knew from back home. She was an old crush, my friend's old girlfriend Karla, looking as great as ever. Unfortunately, she was not alone or with a girlfriend. She was with my naïve classmate Tim, and – another shock – on their honeymoon. The she-wolf had caught her prey.

She said hello, a quick introduction, and before we could chat, they were on her way. But it was enough to remind me that I'd almost lived with Karla when she and my friend invited me to join them in their apartment uptown. When my friend, distraught after their breakup, told me what a big liar she was, I was happy I had declined.

I wanted to see the countryside, so the next day, I took a tour bus to Delphi. The small stone stadium was in surprisingly good condition, in a lovely remote mountain setting, but the Oracle had retired, so the future remained uncertain. As I rode back through the green hills, I imagined floating through the rolling green hills of the New York Hudson Valley, where my parents lived. It annoyed me that here I was in far-away Greece, the cradle of western history and democracy, and I was homesick for the humdrum world I thought I'd finally escaped.

The bus returned to Piraeus at sundown, and I was eager to get back on the ship, like the Greeks many centuries before, for an overnight to Messina, to investigate some of my family legends in Magna Graecia.

To Florence

Roma
ITALY

GREECE

TURKEY

Delphi
Athens

MIDDLE EAST

CYPRUS
LEBANON
SYRIA

2 1

3

Messina

Haifa
Beirut

from KUWAIT

SICILIA

CRETE

ISRAEL
Jerusalem

JORDAN

Mediterranean Sea

TUNISIA

1 Capo d'Orlando
2 Cefalu'
3 Casteltermini

EGYPT

LIBYA

Map 8. Greece from East to West

Magna Graecia

I arrived by boat from Athens to Messina, the Sicilian side of the strait that separates the island from the mainland – Charybdis and Scylla in Homer's Odyssey. I had a limited budget and one year of college Italian. We didn't know any blood relatives left in Sicily, but that wasn't going to stop me. My grandfather had died suddenly of a stroke the year before, and I wanted my first visit to Sicily to be in his honor.

My grandfather, Bernardo Catalinotto, was born in Sicily in 1883 and lived in the village of Santo Stefano for twenty-three years before emigrating to New York. My main goal was to make a pilgrimage to Santo Stefano. I wanted to see what the town was like and to check the hard-to-believe family legend that all my aunts assured me was the God's honest truth – that my *nonno* Bernardo was the seventeenth of twenty-seven children, and the first of only two boys.

The first night in Sicily I shared a cheap hotel room with my new friend Michelle, a tall thin French girl I'd met on the boat. The next day Michelle took the train to Club Med Cefalù. She invited me to visit her, so I said sure, hoping it would be a lively overnight of Parisian partygoers to give me a break from my family visits.

Map 9. Sicily

Family First

I took the train from Messina along Sicily's north shore to nearby Capo d'Orlando to visit my dad's friend John Leone, who had worked with him at Gino-the-Chef's restaurant in New York's Hudson Valley. John was short and thin, with short salt-and-pepper hair. He was a lively old guy, warm and welcoming, about the same age as my father. I felt like I was back home, representing my family to family friends, and getting an insider's glimpse of how people really live in the old country.

John, a widower, lived in a small, detached house a few blocks from the beach. It was a small town and seemed surprisingly familiar, an Italian equivalent to the riverfront town of Cold Spring-on-Hudson, near where my parents had settled. Capo d'Orlando seemed more festive than Cold Spring. Young people rode motor scooters noisily up and down the streets.

The two tall young men chatting next door told me they had just graduated from university in Palermo and looked forward to professional careers with good salaries. They knew my father's young friend, Cono Rinaldi, a local graduate in landscape architecture who worked as a landscape gardener in New York. Cono embodied an intriguing combination of the old Sicily of emigration with the new Sicily of education.

John lived with his daughter's family in a three-generation household like the one I'd grown up in, in Archie Bunker's Queens. His plump daughter dressed in black, like a stereotype of Sicilian women perpetually in mourning. Her husband worked for the state railroad, which the family thought a great job. This fit another stereotype of Southern Italians, to aspire to a civil service post, with job security and a pension.

I thought of his situation with horror. His life seemed a living death: to be married to that unfriendly woman in black with one kid in diapers and another on the way. I thought, no wonder another part of the stereotype is that the married men all have mistresses. Of course, I kept these prejudiced and unkind thoughts to myself.

John took me for a walk along the waterfront south of town to show me his property, a large beachfront parcel with dozens of olive trees and a concrete housing shell. Two of its three stories were enclosed and ready for move-in. The third floor would come later.

I felt a flood of affection and admiration for him. He was such a good guy, putting his hard-earned American money into a house for his children and grandchildren. I looked forward to telling my dad about his friend's project, like the project my dad built when I was a baby, when he moved his parents upstate. Family first.

After dinner under a bright moon and stars, John stood in front of his modest house and pointed out, along the coast on a hill, some lights from what he described as a fancy restaurant with dining and dancing above the sea. I imagined people dressed as in *La Dolce Vita* on the Via Veneto, arriving in their Ferrari's and enjoying the great beauty of the place. I imagined returning to Sicily on holiday, taking my wife or girlfriend to the restaurant with its sea views and dancing. Although I never got to see what it really was like, the distant view of the hillside restaurant overlooking the sea has stayed with me for years.

Quale Santo Stefano

What good luck! The next day I set out on the train to find my grandfather's hometown, and I found it a scant thirty miles west of Capo d'Orlando, a major stop on the rail line. I hadn't realized Santo Stefano was on the sea. What beautiful stonework on the walls next to the steep road that led up to the lovely piazza that overlooked the sea!

I was suddenly curious to find out how a desperately poor town that many had abandoned went through two world wars and had gained such prosperity. I entered city hall and asked the clerk to find a record of my grandfather's birth in 1883. He checked all the records and could not find my grandfather. In fact, he could not find anyone named Catalinotto.

I was puzzled. I said politely in my schoolboy Italian that I was sure he was born in Santo Stefano in Sicily.

He said, "Which Santo Stefano?" *Quale Santo Stefano?*

"How many are there?"

"Seven."

Yikes! Or as my *nonno* used to say: *"Porca miseria!"* (Dirty Misery!)

The clerk was very kind. He asked if I knew anything else about my grandfather's hometown. I said I was surprised to find it here because I thought it was closer to Agrigento. He said in that case he was sure he knew which one it was. Mystery solved. I was in beautiful seaside Santo Stefano di Camastra (SSC) in Messina Province. I needed Santo Stefano Quisquina (SSQ) in the remote hills of Agrigento Province.

L'Esprit du Club

I ran down to the seaside train station and jumped aboard the next westbound train. The train ran surprisingly smoothly through tunnels and along the seacoast and soon pulled into the small beachfront town of Cefalù. I hiked a mile on the dirt road out of town and came upon a large gate surrounded by signs in French. I showed my passport to the gatekeeper and felt like I was crossing a national border to a French island colony when Michelle gave me a kiss on each cheek.

Michelle took me past the thatched huts and down to a beach of fine sand, but no one was lounging naked or even half-naked on the beach. The guests were all out on sailboats and snorkeling. Michelle said she was having a good time and praised the Club's great water sports equipment and lessons. She laughed about the friendly culture, where all the guys were encouraging the women to have *l'esprit du club,* (club spirit) which meant, well, we knew what it meant.

The visit turned out to be more of a pit stop than spring break. I slept alone in the hut I was assigned, and over cappuccino and croissant, we agreed to meet in two weeks in Paris.

Once out of the gate, I was back on the barren rural approach road, with a few old Sicilians tending their sheep. I had suddenly left the first world and re-entered a version of the third world. Because of my ancestry, I felt I had a foot in each.

Scandolino

I hiked to the main highway and lifted my thumb. There wasn't much traffic on the highway, but in a few minutes two friendly French guys in a *deux-chevaux (Citroen 2CV vapeur)* picked me up. I soon learned why they were so welcoming. *Deux chevaux* means two horses. I sat in the back behind the removable front seat, and every time the hill was steep, got out and helped them push the car up the hill. I was the third *cheval*.

Fortunately for my back, we parted ways soon. I took the bus from Termini to Santo Stefano, the real Santo Stefano, and headed for the city clerk's office. The clerk found a treasure trove of birth records of my forefathers and foremothers, including my grandfather Bernardo's birth certificate, dated 1883, and thirteen of his siblings (not the twenty-six of family legend). And yes, only two were boys.

There was also a marriage certificate, but the marriage date was 1876, ten years after my first grand-aunt's birth. I had heard that my great grandfather was a rebel – my aunts swore he had been aide-de-camp to Garibaldi – but had no idea they had four kids at the wedding.

I asked, "*È uno scandolo?*" (Is it a scandal?)

He smiled reassuringly, with thumb and index finger aligned: *"Un scandolino."* (a mini scandal)

The clerk took me on a walking tour up to the main square and pointed out a few forlorn shops where Bernardo, educated as an Italian teacher, might have worked as a shoemaker. The Catalinotto family might have lived opposite, in a large stone house, but the clerk was not sure.

I had asked Nonno about his fifty plus years of life in the USA, and he told me exciting stories of his adventures in Florida and Manhattan. I kicked myself that I had never thought to ask him what his life was like in the twenty-three years before he left his hometown.

Not an Easy Life

After a few hours in Santo Stefano, I got back on the bus to Agrigento. What a Philistine I was! I did not visit the famous ruins of Agrigento. I'd seen ruins in Lebanon and Greece and expected to see more in Rome, so I just changed buses to my next family visit, to my Uncle Tony's brother Carlo in Casteltermini.

Carlo met me at the main square and led me to his shop on the main street, Via Roma. He was a watchmaker and property owner, tall, thin, and a little funny-looking, with the slight clumsiness of an Ichabod Crane. This surprised me, as my Uncle Tony was solid and handsome. I caught a glimpse of his shop and he led me up a narrow stairway to his apartment above the store. We entered a small living room, dark and bare. It contained a large brass bed with a high mattress, occupied by a small sleeping man, Carlo's father, who was eighty-eight years old and gravely ill.

Carlo led me quickly past the patient's bed into the kitchen, which had a view of nearby apartments and distant hills. I recall a full kitchen with refrigerator and stove, but the only appliance I remember clearly was a simple bare toilet in the middle of the room. I tried to conceal my shock and decided not to risk asking him about it in my schoolboy Italian, possibly subject to misunderstanding. Carlo cheerfully told me he had arranged a room for me in a neighbor's apartment. I was relieved.

Later, I explored the town on my own. A large church marked one end of the main street, with the large Communist Party headquarters at the other end. Every evening, the townsfolk took their daily stroll, the *passeggiata*, between these two opposite poles of Sicilian life.

Strolling along the main drag, I heard a group of young men chatting in what just might be English. They were four Londoners, one of whose parents lived in town. The Anglo-Sicilian told me how people made a living in this town. Many rose early to take workers' buses to industrial jobs in the Palermo suburbs, forty miles away, and returned late in the evening. These industrial workers were the mainstay, along with agriculture. Not an easy life.

Carlo took me for a walk to his property outside the town to show me his olive trees, and in the distance, his laborer – on horseback – who worked the farm for a share of the yield. He said this was standard operating procedure in Sicily since Roman times. So, I thought, his tenant is a sharecropper.

Carlo appeared anxious during my entire visit. Perhaps he just wanted to be a good host. After all, he knew I would report my visit to his big brother in New York. I felt sorry for him. There seemed neither wife nor children in his life. He appeared on his own in the world, caring for his elderly, infirm father, and soon to be completely alone.

The next day, after a bus ride to Palermo, I caught the overnight train to Rome. We crossed from Charybdis to Scylla on the train ferry. I sat on my luggage outside the toilet, surrounded by draftees in brown uniforms who called me *l'Americano* and spoke to me kindly, but it was a miserably crowded trip. I forced myself to stay awake in case someone was tempted to lighten the Americano's wallet. Fourteen hours later we reached Rome, where I staggered out into the terminal station to seek a cheap hotel.

to Munich

Maniago

Venezia

Firenze

Roma

Messina

from Greece

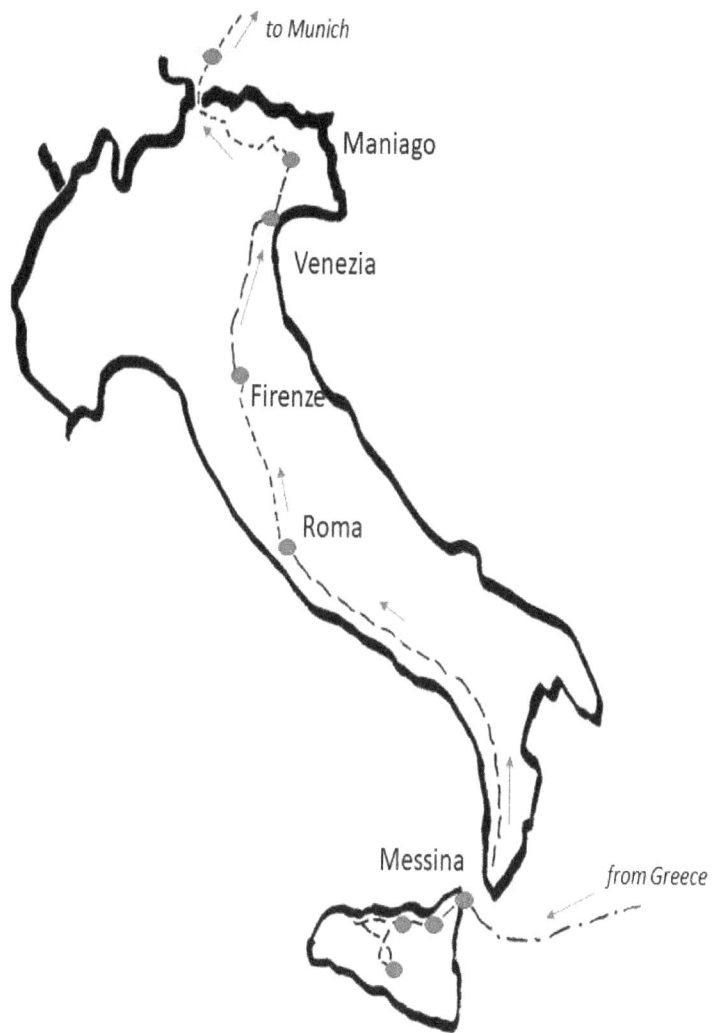

Map 10. Italy from South to North

My Cinema Paradiso

After a few days in Rome, including a visit to the Villa d'Este, I started my trip to Florence at a gas station in the northern suburbs of Rome, near the freeway entrance. I greeted the driver of the coolest car at the gas pumps in my best schoolboy Italian.

"Good day. Is possible, Sir, I can go with you? We go to Florence?"

I was hoping he would be amused for an hour or two chatting with me on an otherwise solitary ride. It worked. His Alfa Romeo sedan was soon cruising at 160 clicks (100 mph – gulp) on the Autostrada del Sole, the sleek expressway that Italian engineering genius built along the country's spine.

He let me off at the Florence South exit. An American family from the Midwest was my next ride. They loved hearing me speak English with their children in their station wagon. They were having a great time driving around Italy. I was happy for them, but their little family clique bored me. I was surprised when, though I was a young man with no current girlfriend, I suddenly promised myself that one day I would return to Florence with my future wife and children.

I stayed in a bed-and-breakfast a block from the Duomo, visited the Uffizi, the statue of David and the Pitti Palace. Although not much of a shopper, I bought the cheapest belt I could find in the leather market. My favorite image was Botticelli's exquisite *Birth of Venus*. I also loved his *Primavera,* especially the nymphs in diaphanous robes, which evoked past and hopefully future romantic moments.

From Florence I splurged on a train to Venice, and from the terminal station took public transport on a *vaporetto* along the Grand Canal. My mom's mother, my grandma Emma, had worked as a babysitter in one of the large houses on the Canal when she was fifteen years old. She had an embroidery drawing of the Grand Canal in a picture frame on the wall of her stark white bedroom in our three-generation household in Queens. Now, in Emma's world, I was thrilled to see the houses on the Grand Canal where she had lived and worked in 1903. Later, I sat on my bed in a large room in the hostel filled with twenty youthful Europeans, gazing through a large window to the mountains. Emma's hometown was my next destination.

The next morning, I boarded the train to Maniago, one hour northeast of Venice in the foothills of the Italian Alps. I told a woman on the train that I was visiting relatives in Maniago for the first time. She asked me for my uncle's name. While I knew it was a small town, I was pleasantly surprised when she said she knew him well. She kindly walked me past the unpaved piazza near the town center to his stone row house.

When he opened the door, my short round Grand Uncle Giovanni shouted, "Ber-NAAR-do," spread his arms wide, and gave me a big garlic-scented hug. I felt at home.

Map 11. Northern Italy – Austria

I felt like I was in an Italian movie. But it wasn't pretend. He was genuinely happy to see me and I him. My grandma, his big sister, had been like a second mother to me. She helped raise me and had died two years earlier.

Giovanni was the youngest of the seven siblings and the only one who had stayed in Maniago. He had last seen his sister well over fifty years earlier, when Emma emigrated with her sisters to London to work as a hotel maid, met my grandfather Otto, a waiter from Vienna, and one step ahead of Otto's Austrian draft board, re-emigrated with him to New York.

Emma and five of her siblings, driven by poverty, had left their homes and migrated to London, where all but one re-migrated to Western Canada, Australia, and New York – all over the rapidly industrializing countries of the English-speaking world. It always amazed and saddened me that although they kept in touch with annual letters and occasional photos, they never saw one another for the rest of their lives.

I had arrived (no surprise) at dinnertime. It was the day of the first U.S. manned space flight, so the TV had a seat at the dinner table. My relatives were in awe. This was 1965, during the Cold War. Much of the local economy was driven by the nearby American airbase at Aviano. Giovanni's son worked there, a good job with security and a pension, the northern Italian equivalent of my father's friend John Leone's son-in-law in Capo d'Orlando.

Giovanni showed me around town and snuck me into the booth at the movie theater. He was the projectionist. I know now what movie we were in. It was *Cinema Paradiso,* a famous Italian movie whose protagonist, after a long absence, returns to his hometown and fondly recalls his friendship with the projectionist who snuck him into the cinema and taught him to operate the films.

Maniago was and still is famous for the manufacture of cutlery. Giovanni took me to the factory and got me a huge discount on a gorgeous set of kitchen shears, knives, and scissors in a dark blue velvet box for my mother, who proudly brandished them at family dinners for the rest of her life.

After two days in Maniago, I was ready to move on. I was hitch-hiking on a rural road just outside of town. I was starting to lose hope, with my thumb outstretched and the late afternoon storm clouds rolling in, when a yellow VW bug pulled over. I was thankful for the ride – I wouldn't have to slink back to Uncle Giovanni's house in Maniago – and overjoyed at the riders. Two German sisters cheerfully welcomed me. I squeezed into the back of the Bug, wishing I were squeezed between the sisters. I was back on the road and ready for misadventure.

Across the Dolomites

At the wheel was 24-year-old Greta, who taught high school English in Munich. Younger sister Alexandra was nineteen. She did not speak English or was too shy to try. They were returning from a week on the Adriatic and hoped to make it home by midnight. Greta lit up when she learned I was a New York native. She asked me to sing the songs I'd learned growing up. I started with my Halsey Junior High and Jamaica High School anthems, moved on to Christmas carols and regressed to nursery rhymes.

In Bolzano we learned that the direct route through the tunnel was snowed in. Greta did not mind. She moved me on to pop songs. I deconstructed the lyrics to Hound Dog and explained how it might feel to be a one-eyed cat peeping through a seafood store. We shook, rattled, and rolled through the Dolomites and over the border.

At ten pm we stopped at a cozy lodge in the Austrian hills. I was hoping to finally get a chance to get to know Alexandra, but Greta swept her off to their room. The baby sister, it was clear, was not going to be teaching me German or anything else that evening. But how could I complain when Greta was paying for my room?

Greta invited me to stay at her family's home in the suburbs. The sisters lived with their parents, and I was invited to dinner with the older generation. In Italy I'd jumped at the chance to have a good dinner with local people my parents' age and find out what they were really like, but I knew too much about the war. I thought about my ex-girlfriend's father, who worked as a cutter in the garment industry and had numbers burnt on his arm. I couldn't enjoy small talk with the same people whose army would have killed many of my friends had they won.

I took a trolley to the city center. They had rebuilt the old destroyed buildings exactly as they were before the war. I shivered when I thought we might pass the site of Hitler's 1923 beer hall putsch, where it all started.

I booked a sleeper on the train to Paris and bunked with a cheerful older French couple who shared their peasant bread and cheese. They were so sweet and such a relief. When they slept, they sent me waves of body odor and over-ripe cheese that kept my nose under the covers all night. I didn't mind and fell fast asleep. **The conductor called out Gare de l'Est at sunrise.**

Back in Paris

After nine months in the Middle East, I was finally back in Paris. My best friend Bob, who last September bought me onion soup at four a.m. in les Halles Centrales, was gone. He'd fled back to the states to marry my old girlfriend. Good luck with that. Our buddy Sam stayed all year, but he was out of town, so I was on my own.

But not all my luck was bad. The foreign students were on summer break, so I got a cheap dorm room at Cité Universitaire. Plus, Sam's fiancé left my semester's mail with her mother, who invited me to lunch. The next morning, I took the local train to her mother's posh suburb and knocked on the front door of her single-family house. I looked forward to meeting a middle-class Parisian lady, hoping for *coq au vin* and a challenging immersion for my schoolboy French.

The lady who answered was short with thin face and lips. A few words of welcome and she quietly led me to the living room. She directed me to a hard-backed chair and placed before me a small table that looked like my dad's old TV tray. She set a large dinner plate on the tray. No *coq*, no *vin*. Just a small hot dog and no bread.

I didn't take it personally, how could I? I thought it might be an expression of disdain for her American future son-in-law, or maybe it was yesterday's leftovers. I wolfed it down and thanked her for the bundle of mail.

Back on the train I ripped open the letter from Selective Service. The clerk, writing from the bare second floor office with a close view of the rumbling Jamaica Avenue El, confirmed that my deferment would end in a few weeks. I took the metro to the Sorbonne, extended my student visa, and sent a copy to the clerk back home. Fingers crossed, another reprieve.

On my last night I was on my way to a party. Normally, I'd have been delighted to see the Parisian girl I'd met in Sicily and the challenge of a French immersion evening, but Susan from Boston College told me it was her last night in Paris after junior year abroad and she wanted to spend it memorably. At last! It was ice cold in my room at Cité Universitaire – I don't remember much else – but I managed to leave Paris smiling.

Home

The charter plane took fourteen hours to fly to JFK. I sat next to Steve, an aeronautical engineer. He said he knew all the sounds an engine makes before it fails and plunges the plane into the sea. I accepted his offer of a sleeping pill and slept through stops in Iceland and Gander. As we landed, Steve told me he'd been up the entire flight. Listening.

On the way home from the airport, my dad took me for a cholesterol feast to the Croton Diner which was his favorite breakfast all day diner on Route 9A in Peekskill, where we both had French toast, scrambled eggs, sausage, bacon and maple syrup and large cups of black coffee. When he lit up a cigar, I knew I was home. At home my mom – my most loyal correspondent – gave me a wet-eyed hug and asked about my new accent with the liquid L's and my plans for staying out of Viet Nam. I assured her I'd lose the accent soon and was thinking about grad school.

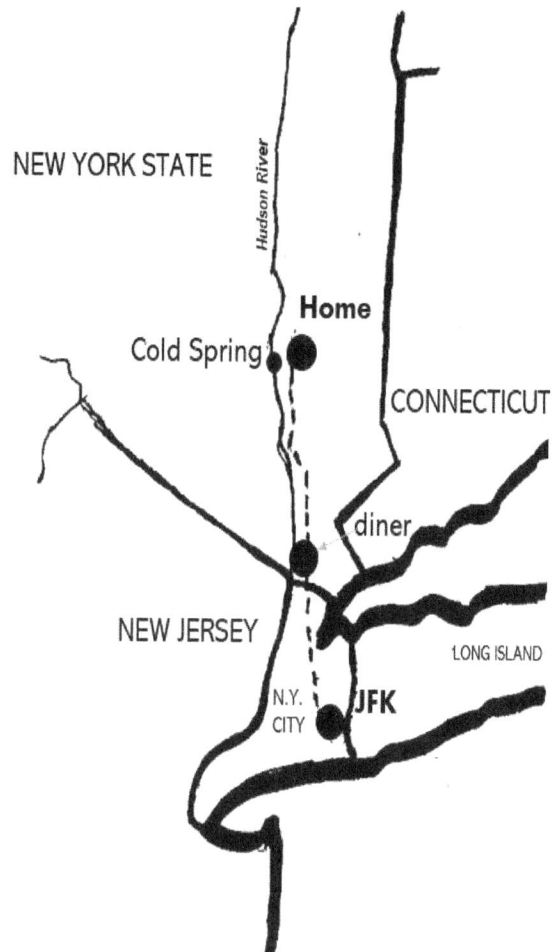

Map 12. New York State

Translations

2. My Battle of Jericho.

Dialogue with taxi driver

I asked politely, "min fadlak, yallah, nrooh, nurjah lil Quds."

  "Please, O God (let's go), we go, we return to al-Quds (Jerusalem)."

He became angry and said, "Inta lil Israliyeen!"

    "You are for the Israelis!"

I said simply, "Areed an irjah lil Quds."

  "I want that I return to al-Quds."

[He asks for more money; I reject his offer]

I told him, "Yallah, nrooh al mahatat il bolees, wa natakellam wiyahoom hinaak."

"Let's go, we go to the station of the police, and we talk with them there."

In the Police Station

I said "Huwa yagool il-shay hiya mish saahaah."

  "He says the thing it is not truth." [i.e., he is lying.]

I asked the police, "Wayn al mahattat il awtoboos?"

    "Where [is] the station [of] the bus?"

3. I am a Spy

Flashback: Discussion with Syrian in restaurant in Kuwait

I said, "Vous avez raison, je suis un espion."

  "You have reason [are right], I am a spy."

8. Quale Santo Stefano

In Santo Stefano di Camastra, speaking with the town clerk.

I said..." Sono sicuro che lui era nato in Santo Stefano."

"I am sure that he was born in Santo Stefano."

He said, "Quale Santo Stefano?"

"Which Santo Stefano?"

I said, "Quanti ci sono?"

"How many are there?"

He said, "Sette."

"Seven."

I said, "Porca miseria!"

"Dirty misery!"

12. Cinema Paradiso.

At the gas station just outside Rome.

I greeted the driver, "Buon giorno. È possibile, Signore, posso andare con Lei? Andiamo a Firenze?"

"Good morning. Is it possible, Sir, I can go with You? We go to Florence?"

About the Author

Bernard Catalinotto is a native New Yorker who upon graduation in 1964, was persuaded by an Oxford Economics Professor turned entrepreneur to work the next year in the Middle East, in the booming newly independent, master planned oil kingdom of Kuwait.

Upon return, he got a master's degree in urban planning, studied a year on a Fulbright in Italy, and worked two more years in the Middle East on the largest construction project since the pyramids. He moved to the San Francisco Bay Area, where he worked on international planning projects before deciding to do his traveling virtually.

He learned mapping and GIS (geographic information systems) and persuaded the owners at Thomas Bros Maps to hire him to manage their major projects and computerize their maps. For the past ten years, he has been publishing community maps in the Bay Area. He also invented and patented a new mapping system for public safety that he is working to deploy.

Still in love with languages, he facilitates Italian and French conversation clubs at the Mill Valley Public Library and continues to dabble in other languages.

Proud of his family, he considers himself a lucky man, hikes every day, lives happily with his wife in Mill Valley, California, has two fine sons, two wonderful daughters-in-law and (so far) two brilliant and extremely cute grandchildren.

www.ingramcontent.com/pod-product-compliance
Lightning Source LLC
Chambersburg PA
CBHW081549040426

42448CB00015B/3260